SANTINO MARELLA

BY JASON BRICKWEG

BELLWETHER MEDIA · MINNEAPOLIS, MN

Are you ready to take it to the extreme?
Torque books thrust you into the action-packed world
of sports, vehicles, mystery, and adventure. These books
may include dirt, smoke, fire, and dangerous stunts.
WARNING: read at your own risk.

Library of Congress Cataloging-in-Publication Data

Brickweg, Jason.
 Santino Marella / by Jason Brickweg.
   p. cm. -- (Torque: Pro wrestling champions)
 Includes bibliographical references and index.
 Summary: "Engaging images accompany information about Santino Marella. The combination of
high-interest subject matter and light text is intended for students in grades 3 through 7"--Provided by
publisher.
 ISBN 978-1-60014-904-7 (hardcover : alk. paper)
1. Marella, Santino, 1979---Juvenile literature. 2. Wrestlers--Canada--Biography--Juvenile literature. I. Title.
 GV1196.M368B75 2013
 796.812092--dc23
 [B]   2012041592

This edition first published in 2013 by Bellwether Media, Inc.

No part of this publication may be reproduced in whole or in part without written permission of the
publisher. For information regarding permission, write to Bellwether Media, Inc., Attention: Permissions
Department, 5357 Penn Avenue South, Minneapolis, MN 55419.

The images in this book are reproduced through the courtesy of: Devin Chen, front cover, pp. 5, 9,
12-13, 14, 16, 18-19, 20-21; Associated Press, pp. 4-5; Zuma Press/Newscom, pp. 7, 10-11, 19;
Dan Harr/AdMedia/Newscom, p. 8; Getty Images, p. 15; AP Images for WWE, pp. 16-17.

CONTENTS

WARNING!

The wrestling moves used in this book are performed
by professionals. Do not attempt to reenact any
of the moves performed in this book.

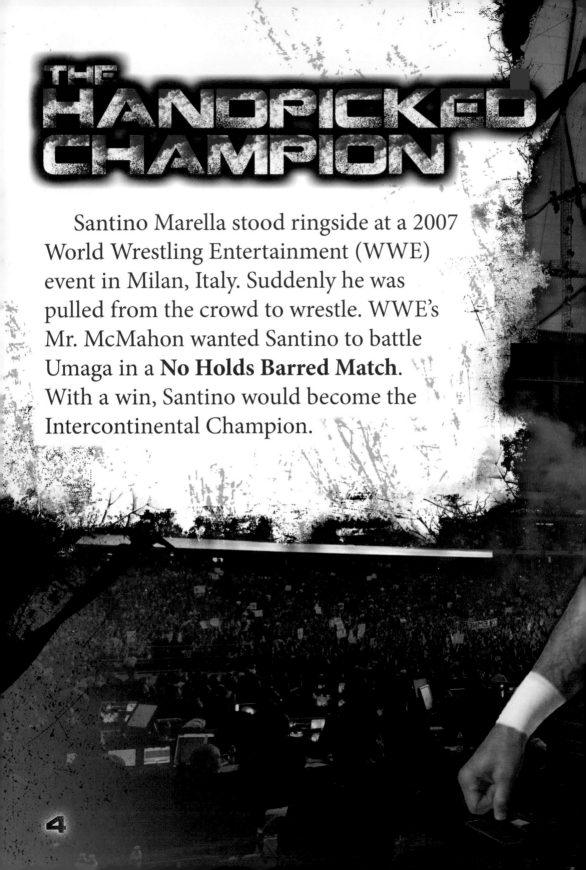

THE HANDPICKED CHAMPION

Santino Marella stood ringside at a 2007 World Wrestling Entertainment (WWE) event in Milan, Italy. Suddenly he was pulled from the crowd to wrestle. WWE's Mr. McMahon wanted Santino to battle Umaga in a **No Holds Barred Match**. With a win, Santino would become the Intercontinental Champion.

Santino delivered a few blows early in the match. After that he took a brutal beating. Umaga was about to jump from the top rope when Bobby Lashley entered the ring. Lashley fought Umaga with his bare hands and then a metal chair. He performed a **Spear** to bring Umaga to the mat. Then he positioned Santino for the pin and the win. With a little help, the handpicked fan defeated the Samoan Bulldozer!

QUICK HIT!

This championship win earned Santino his nickname, the "Milan Miracle."

SANTINO

UMAGA

Anthony Carelli was born on March 14, 1979 in Ontario, Canada. He became a wrestling fan at a young age. He attended shows with his father. At 9 years old, Carelli started training in **judo**. He competed in wrestling tournaments during high school.

After finishing school, Carelli moved to Japan to do **mixed martial arts**. Several years later he moved to the United States to learn to be a professional wrestler. He trained in a small league called Ohio Valley Wrestling (OVW).

Carelli first wrestled in OVW under the ring name Johnny Geo Basco. This name soon changed to Boris Alexiev. WWE offered Carelli a **developmental contract** in 2006. He claimed the OVW Television Championship twice in 2007.

13

BECOMING A CHAMPION

QUICK HIT!

In 2009, Santino dressed as a woman to compete against the WWE divas. He was crowned Miss WrestleMania.

In 2007, Carelli made his WWE **debut** as a fan named Santino Marella. He won the Intercontinental Championship in his very first match. Not long afterward, Santino changed from a **face** to a **heel**. He became the Intercontinental Champion again in 2008. Then he tried to break the record for the longest **reign**. William Regal crushed his hopes a few months later.

Santino formed a **tag team** with Vladimir Kozlov in 2010. They captured the Tag Team Championship that year. Then in late 2011, Santino focused on chasing singles titles. The next year he faced Jack Swagger for the United States Championship and won.

VLADIMIR KOZLOV

DIVING
HEADBUTT

Santino is an entertainer in the ring. Many of his **signature moves** show his goofy personality. He often performs the Diving Headbutt. For this move, he drives his head into an opponent's body by falling on top of him. Santino is also known to do the splits during some moves.

COBRA STRIKE

Santino's **finishing move** is truly unique. He imitates a cobra snake with his hand. Then the "cobra" strikes his opponent in the throat. The Cobra Strike allows Santino to put on a show before attacking. He brings a little fun to every fight!

GLOSSARY

debut—a first appearance

developmental contract—an agreement in which a wrestler signs with WWE but then wrestles in smaller leagues to gain experience and develop skills

face—a wrestler seen by fans as a hero

finishing move—a wrestling move meant to finish off an opponent so that he can be pinned

heel—a wrestler seen by fans as a villain

judo—a martial art that focuses on throwing or taking down an opponent

mixed martial arts—a full-contact sport that allows punching, kicking, and many other fighting techniques

No Holds Barred Match—a wrestling match that allows the use of weapons and outside interference; a wrestler cannot be disqualified from a No Holds Barred Match.

reign—the time during which a person holds a title or position of power

signature moves—moves that a wrestler is famous for performing

Spear—a move in which a wrestler charges and dives at a standing opponent, driving his shoulder into the opponent's stomach

tag team—two wrestlers who compete as a team

TO LEARN MORE

AT THE LIBRARY

Black, Jake. *The Ultimate Guide to WWE*. New York, N.Y.: Grosset & Dunlap, 2011.

Price, Sean Stewart. *The Kids' Guide to Pro Wrestling*. Mankato, Minn.: Edge Books, 2012.

Roemhildt, Mark. *Jack Swagger*. Minneapolis, Minn.: Bellwether Media, 2012.

ON THE WEB

Learning more about Santino Marella is as easy as 1, 2, 3.

1. Go to www.factsurfer.com.

2. Enter "Santino Marella" into the search box.

3. Click the "Surf" button and you will see a list of related Web sites.

With factsurfer.com, finding more information is just a click away.

INDEX